For Melanie and Megan

First Edition

"The Hippopotamus Song" by Donald Swann and Michael Flanders,
© 1952 and 1970, Chappell & Co., a division of Warner/Chappell Music, Inc.
All rights reserved. Used by permission.

Library of Congress Cataloging-in-Publication Data

Flanders, Michael.
  The hippopotamus song: a muddy love story / words by Michael Flanders; music by
Donald Swann and Michael Flanders; illustrated by Nadine Bernard Westcott.
—1st ed.
      p.   cm.
  Summary: Lovestruck hippos and their muddy escapades provide
inspiration for a humorous song. Music included with book.
  ISBN 0-316-28557-9
  [1. Hippopotamus—Songs and music. 2. Songs.] I. Swann, Donald, 1923–.
II. Westcott, Nadine Bernard, ill. III. Title.
PZ8.3.F37Hi   1991
782.42164'0268—dc20   90-39797

Joy Street Books are published by Little, Brown and Company (Inc.)

10 9 8 7 6 5 4 3 2 1

HR

Published simultaneously in Canada by
Little, Brown & Company (Canada) Limited

Printed in the United States of America

The
Hippopotamus
Song

♥ A Muddy Love Story ♥

The Hippopotamus

Joy Street Books
Little, Brown and Company
Boston   Toronto   London

Song
♥ A Muddy Love Story ♥

Words by Michael Flanders
Music by Donald Swann and Michael Flanders
Illustrated by Nadine Bernard Westcott

A bold Hippopotamus was standing one day
On the banks of the cool Shalimar.
He gazed at the bottom as it peacefully lay
By the light of the evening star.

Away on the hill top sat combing her hair
His fair Hippopotamine maid.
The Hippopotamus was no ignoramus
And sang her this sweet serenade.

Mud! Mud! Glorious mud!
Nothing quite like it for cooling the blood.
So, follow me, follow, down to the hollow,
And there let us wallow in glorious mud.

The fair Hippopotama he aimed to entice,
From here seen on the hill top above,
As she hadn't got a ma to give her advice,
Came tiptoeing down to her love.

Like thunder the forest re-echoed the sound
Of the song that they sang as they met.
His enamorata adjusted her garter
And lifted her voice in duet.

Mud! Mud! Glorious mud!
Nothing quite like it for cooling the blood.
So, follow me, follow, down to the hollow,
And there let us wallow in glorious mud.

Now more Hippopotami began to convene
On the banks of that river so wide.
I wonder now what am I to say of the scene
That ensued by the Shalimar side?

They dived all at once with an ear-splitting splash,
Then rose to the surface again,
A regular army of Hippopotami
All singing this haunting refrain.

Mud! Mud! Glorious mud!
Nothing quite like it for cooling the blood.

So, follow me, follow, down to the hollow,
And there let us wallow in glorious mud.

The Hippopotamus Song

Words by **Michael Flanders**
Music by **Donald Swann and Michael Flanders**
Illustrated by **Nadine Bernard Westcott**

Voice

Piano

A
bold Hip-po-pot-a-mus was stand-ing one day On the banks of the cool Sha-li-mar.
fair Hip-po-pot-a-ma he aimed to en-tice, From here seen on the hill top a-bove,
more Hip-po-pot-a-mi be-gan to con-vene On the banks of that riv-er so wide.

He gazed at the bot-tom as it peace-ful-ly lay By the light of the e-ven-ing star.
As she had-n't got a ma to give her ad-vice, Came — tip-toe-ing down to her love.
I won-der now what am I to say of the scene That en-sued by the Sha-li-mar side?